Study for Necessity

Winner of the Iowa Poetry Prize

Study for Necessity

POEMS BY

JoEllen Kwiatek

UNIVERSITY OF IOWA PRESS, *Iowa City*

University of Iowa Press, Iowa City 52242
Copyright © 2015 by JoEllen Kwiatek
www.uiowapress.org
Printed in the United States of America

Design by Barbara Haines

The University of Iowa Press is a member of Green Press Initiative and is committed to preserving
natural resources.

Printed on acid-free paper

Library of Congress Cataloging-in-Publication Data
Kwiatek, JoEllen, 1957–
[Poems. Selections]
Study for necessity : poems / by JoEllen Kwiatek.
pages   cm. —(Iowa poetry prize)
ISBN 978-1-60938-324-4 (pbk), ISBN 978-1-60938-325-1 (ebk)
I. Title.
PS3561.W48A6   2015

811'.54–dc23   2014034809

For Odile
1914–2002
——

This spring has just ended and will never return.
Everything will be known in the winter.
—LUDVIK VACULIK

CONTENTS

ACKNOWLEDGMENTS

"*Landscape as Language*," "Low Tide," "The Overseer," "A Walk in Daylight," "Miles to Go," "Another World," "A Delicate Thing," "*A Sad and Human Face*," "What's a Start?," "Snowlight," "Sea Below Rocks," and "*For Lo, I Come at Noonday*," all appeared in *The American Poetry Review.* "In the Country," "Daphne," and "Madonna del Parto" appeared in *ForPoetry.com.* "August Burial" and "Victoriana" appeared in *Stone Canoe.* Thank you to the editors of these publications.

Deepest thanks to Paul Aviles, Michael Burkard, Barbara Farah, Sheila Gillooly, Karen Fish, Susan Jones, and Aida Khalil for their sterling friendship, and also to my family, the Kwiateks, Foxs, Heinzs, Burns, Adamcyzks and Bouchers, for their love and support.

To Reverend Judy Breny, *thank you.*

Thanks also to SUNY Oswego, to friends and colleagues in the English and Creative Writing Department, especially Maureen Curtin, Brad Korbesmeyer, Robert O'Connor, Donna Steiner, and Leigh Wilson. And to my students, thanks and love.

Finally, I am indebted to the University of Iowa, to James McCoy, Susan Hill Newton, Allison Means, Karen Copp, Clare Jones, and everyone at the University of Iowa Press.

Study for Necessity

Sea Below Rocks

What does the sea see—? Something
awful. It has the roving
thwarted glance of a mare in blinders,
something awful facing her stall.

Petrified, swaybacked, the sea
jerks on its tether but
remains facing the rocks— vision
is a bridle, something

worn until it's threadbare, like
the mystery of a thing
worn to brightness— rain or stone.

Landscape as Language

I took the funicular
to the top, almost.
A kind of dying
amplification,
like evening
but not, rode
with me. Wood-
lands passed
under my feet. So
high above, I saw
their crowns, like
crocuses. The note
I was looking for
was held
repressively, as it
is in certain per-
fumes until sudden heat
or cold. How
positive the cold air seemed,
removing the log from my eyes.

Caspar David Friedrich
has fled the snowy
city in patent leather
boots. Wherefore, where
to— unknown.

For Lo, I Come at Noonday

First— the tiny, explosively
deserted instant of *before*;
then— in the sky, the same
smoking badge of light, wash
of a neighbor's still on the line . . .

No going back to the house or
crashing through the coarse fields.
The air is dark as an ice hole, dark
and bright, for a long time.

for Jane Kenyon

The Overseer

Into late late
late summer,
fall comes
with its stirrup,
its bronze light.

In the middle
of the road
or field, it
doesn't move.

The cicada
is down to
embers, the leaves
are chapped . . .

Still, it won't
move. Though
mention is every-
where on the estate.

Daphne

A many-leaved hesitance
focused me. The leaves
blew, rashly. The drift
accumulated, spoke by spoke . . .

How else to see, through
shining tiers, the charged
disheveled flyway?

Low Tide

The strangenesses
are plenty
here— up
stalks, roving
the water-mashed
ground. Crabs
& feline
insects, their
trembling is
peripheral.
Huge & close,
the dark blue
sky hovers
like a gleaner's
back, inches from
the marsh. Of
the several
kinds of thought,
two are here:
dwellers &
itinerants hiding, seeking.

Victoriana

I took a nap
in the sea,
in the bright water, coddled
by smithereens of brightness.

Dark as a vole, accordion-
pleated— that's how I
thought of consciousness,
as a *thing* from another era.

A Walk in Daylight

Not the end,
Count, but
the rich middle.
Dark as pines
in the schloss,
a frail immediacy
lighting the hour,
the rockface. A
visitor would be
grotesque.
          Someone
like yourself— belated,
repercussive, comb-
ing the fire. Out
of thrall to any
clues beside the way—
haphazard, unaligned:
the invisible figurative
like blowdown trumpeting
a storm. The storm's
passing.
          In these mountains,
cool's impounded in
the walls like a secret.
Sunlight is a studio, a
sanatorium. The glacier
has a shelf life. Whoever
seeks abroad may find
it.

Log:

For some weeks I lay
in the crevasse
hallucinating. It
was my own hand
in front of my face
passing the time.
The cold was heavier
than a major appliance;
I was soldered to it
as to an inner life.
The glassy field I
almost crossed, touch-
ing the sea, vanished—
I forgot to look down.
The voyage grows more
& more captivating. More terse.

A Sad and Human Face
—Odilon Redon

The swamp flower, a sad
and human face, retrieves
the moon, its fog of self-
expunging light glowing.

The artist was a strange
one to draw this lamp
with a broken swing— I
intuit that it's broken—
this strange planet reading
the water.

      In the backwoods
of the universe, thick-
ankled, preposterous,
the swamp flower is waiting
like any donor.

Lieutenant Trakl

Silently, God opens his golden eyes
over the place of skulls.

—Georg Trakl

I let the plains go— stomped
like fire all the twined
grasses   Memory
bellowed   The vantage
bled   Wide as relief or desolation

Another World

The long adjournment to evening
commences. The long slow drink
of detachment. It's summer, and
loss is sweet. A thousand
distillations commingle. A
thousand trees. The finish
to something uncanny or un-
necessary, someone's voluptuous
deserted tact. Mercy
of the large trees, torches
blown out by the opening dimness.

Summerlude

Eyedeep in the lake,
the surface trembl-
ing, dark as a revolver,

the cold of it slipping
cold shoes on my feet . . . Look

up, look up— Fresh horses
are coming. All I
don't know racing the sun.

for Aida Khalil

Return of Orpheus

Because I could not see, I
looked. I saw you vanish
into a look. How you shone
wherever I turned. Fine
as a hair singled out by a thrill.

Archeology

Unearthable light
of pain— torso
of a god, a stone

calved by the underworld . . .

Nothing to put away or go
on with down there

Orpheus Singing

It was a bright spar
that dipped & lolled
on the water . . . Isolate

as shepherds' fires, each
hour from the others . . . How

cold the spellbinding was/how
spellbinding the cold . . . I

struck the water's insular
gong from change to change, regardless.

A Lack of Brooding Shone

Canoed the horizon— hard
chest, radium
of twilight— for disrepairs,

another feeling, more stately,
varnished— another daring
retreat. Retreat is a lamp
held steady . . . steady.

Headache

Double rose of noon, brilliant
dark of the hallway:
left— right— left—
soldier, recluse.

Circling the floor
a ball bearing
can be slow, slow
as a thought
on the spur of, on
the ceiling the ghostly
amber tree where my
colonel hanged himself.

Report to the King

I died in the chrysanthemum
forest, the pungent brightness
skittering over me, strobe
after strobe. I took it hard—
in the sternum— like the rowing geese.

What's a Start?

                        A reverie,
local and momentous, hard
to put your foot in twice
or once;
a movement as of water on
top of water, inchoate
while perishing . . .
                        The surface appears
riddled with detours that
recur mysteriously.
Winking like the glaucous belly
of an early star, except
at evening when the water turns,
for a while, to lotion. All
labor turns reclusive. Like
the many-layered underneath:

uninterrupted, forested.

The Find

A token of strangeness—
the dark material
of a bonnet
lying in the rough
sharp grass of high
summer . . . the mortally
wounded past. How
small the bonnet
face. How pelvic
narrow. Fallen
out of the bright closet of noon.

Song of Experience

Severed from the tree,
the sky flew— a
concave, bright
depressurizing, a queer
high speed assailed
by luster— *I*
was angry with my friend.
A small tight rain
was falling, damp-
ening the tough grass where my astonishment lay. All
around it
the invisible countryside.

A Cold Shine

A cold shine is
on this fruit,
hand-held, un-
perfectly steady.

Let the bough
bend, the gold-
en apple sink in
the grass— like
the hours, like a
swan— mellow & cold.

Snowlight

The mind's a lonesome flourish,
stark as deviation's
branch before the snow,
a dark cabin ogled by snowlight.

Crossing the hacked up sea
of snow, the moon
waist-high, lunging and
capitulating, addressed by
resources that make no sound.

A Delicate Thing

Ah sister! Desolation
is a delicate thing.
 —Percy Bysshe Shelley

The woods are full
of relics, toppled
gestures, deposed
   ideas.
      Imagination's
banked in a crevice,
sponged by leaves,
humus, quiet.

. . . The staying power,

where the soil's been
churned, of a mess
of leaves, one
like a black silk glove

face down on the path.

Face down or aside, going
   below
the derailed stream or
above . . . to the lot. The trees

there are like men, though
not walking.
            Neither

are you—
        Stock still,

invisible, drifted
from the open
where, hushed
by cold, paddles lifted for
the glide forward on faint
intuition
        beneath those trees . . .

Muse

Walking is a process
of waiting, waiting
is a process of effort,
effort is the secret
of interment— the kiss in the dark,
the cooling dark seal.

In *The New York Times*

Two years in a cell
alone, *riddled with
disease, encrust-
ed with sores, and
bloated with
tumors,* at ten years
old in 1795
the Dauphin dies.

Like a face inch-
close, the wall
of terra incognita
came at me at
tunnel-speed
— then pulled away.

for Reverend Judy Breny

Changed

I drove bewildered on
& on. Through gates
without dominion.
The look of things— mute,
processional, changed—
was misleading. No
deliberate residence
or grave news to learn
there. I focused on
the tablet of the sky.
Blue is the color
of deoxygenation, of rarity.

Day for Night

Over my head the iron
bell of clairvoyance
shivers. The weeds
shiver— & the sun,
torn up like a weed
& tossed over the horizon— *What book*

what book shall I read now— I don't know.

Planet

One hand covering
my eyes, an arm
circling my
belly, his
knee punching the backs
of mine, Sleep
restrained me. My night-

gown stretched like a sound. Glisten-

ing, trembly, my own
dreams were held
up to me like a spoon. For
a second I lost
consciousness— unmined, un-
shone, unswerving
planet— before waking again on the ward.

Drinking Up

I put my cheek against
Charlotte Brontë's. I
had to stop there
on the moor. Heights

of wind & wet smote
our laughter— a
dark mirrory finish
with a silver bloom. Night

after night slammed down like a tankard.

Growing

Tore up the damask
conifers, the rak-
ish sound of fuel—

a rip, a long
wandering assessment

of the middle of my
life— one

thought after another
growing hair like a rope.

Thaw

I made peace. I
signed the document. All
my generals, dead. Authority
striding into a cloud. Gangrene.
Crows. Runoff gushing down the matted hillsides.

To Autumn

A forest was my studio,
everlasting, dim.
Spiked by the radiance
of fallout— *belle indifférence.*

I had no faith, Lord, I had
no Lord but you.

With rocks & stones & trees
I will famish likelihood, I thought.

The Hermit

Blood on cold
victuals, the hermit
eats alone. The rock
is his lair. Whether
yea or no. Leaning
far into the rock— ocean
or bone.

Looking at Early Photographs

They are strangely jointed—
I think of roots— in their
powder-dusted, elbow-punched
clothes. Ill at ease. Ill.

They look out as if seeing
were a form of radiant
isolation, leafless
as the sea and
like the sea, a fisher of men.

In the Country

1

Nights of reading
fed my seriousness.
The print bulged,
heavy with sap.
The sap glowed. Trees
of my youth and
the sun through them . . .

2

        Helmless
dusk enters the yard
to the sound of bath
water. The dim water,
the porcelain parlor,
luminously cool . . . From
its single high prisoner's
window, the moon looks
out. Down the listing
corridor— we used to joke
handrails were needed—
the top, the very tops
of the trees were blowing like a gate.

3

In Chekov, in spring,
nothing happens for the first time.

for Kate Stapleton

August Burial

Make haste slowly
under the sun, bower
of hallucination— *I*
die because I am not dying.

. . . Form of the dark
pine, a towering
dress of dark bees.

for Susan Jones

Urn Lake

Autumn with the moon
and sheaves of the moon,

phosphor of diminish-
 ment's long

shank— as if the cold
 attraction of

antagonism propelled light
 and objects

apart— *Lord, it is time.*
 Lay the compress

of unburied haste, of in-
 ward grown

preoccupation, the fogged
 glow of latency

on the botched yield. Let
 directness

die, Lord, shriveled
 like a grudge. Use

is over. From chasm to
 chasm, watch

the glorious sorrows fall.

for Karen Fish

Cloak

Out of the sun's
stable my
horse ran
darkening the field. Home-

less exaltation bearing my voice.

Wheatfield with Crows

Gorged on the sun, the sustenance lieth
tarnishing in the field, in the field. Deep

as the cry of a horn, your illness, your
labor. *Found with him*, your brother wrote

on the draft of a letter to himself. The cure
for almost anything was sourceless, like the sun.

for Paul Aviles

Madonna del Parto

My vigilance steadied
like a tear. It
coats the sky, the bare
shin of propinquity;

formal and desolating
as curfew or
the garden of the daylight

moon: *no ocean, no trespass.*

for Donna Marsh O'Connor

Ryder, Albert Pinkham

The dark woods shone
with a mineral
radiance— deep, deep.

All day they've stood
at the end of the field like a horse.

Miles to Go

Slow driver, the moon's
bonked headlight
sniffing the way
for miles . . . Longevity
is delicate, the wind-
shield glowing, the snow
fainting, again and again.

Dear K—

So the help goes away again,
without helping.
                              —Franz Kafka

No one is coming. Zig-
zagging thru
the concourse. If you
raise them, his hat
bobs for leagues in your
binoculars . . . Dear
K—, the hour
is coming
to wean the subject
of coming &
going. There, on
the road, to see
one he used . . . Dear
K—, for the hour
has come. Pared
from duration—
the long high whistle of duration.

for Michael Burkard

Horse & Train

Night-gleam
of the horse
on the rails   Doom

shies   like snow there

I have turpentine
in my lungs

Iron paint

Strong, stronger than

for Barbara Farah

Lazarus

Now you are ready to walk
with me. I should close
my eyes for the meteor
of seconds, the trans-
migration of loss into gold.
Gold of the body coming
forward. The inmate, the marrow.

for Sheila Gillooly Greene

How Long Do You Mean to Be Content?

—his doppelganger to Shelley

Whose inner-
ness, Mein
Herr, whose
sleeve enamel-
ed with tar?
Who's drowned
but clairvoyant—
the reader. The reader.

Mine

This light is loss backward.
—Louise Bogan

l will change for you,
said Evening. l will
take off my clothes
when you appear
on the tundra . . . I'll

be the last one and
you'll be the last
one to see the other.
I'll cross over to you

of necessity; for as
long as it takes,
the light is a tunnel,
the earth a gold mine.

Answer

I took no for
an answer. I
took it & took it—
more wood
for the stove— more!
more!— until the fire
grew like a tree in Paradise.

NOTES

"*For Lo, I Come at Noonday,*" the title is from the Shaker hymn Jane Kenyon used as an epigraph to "Part IV" of her book *Constance*.

"To Autumn," the phrase "with rocks & stones & trees" is taken from William Wordsworth's poem, "A Slumber Did My Spirit Seal."

"Report to the King" and "Mine" are indebted to Jean Valentine's poems "Barrie's Dream, the Wild Geese" and "The River at Wolf," respectively.

"*Song of Experience*" refers to William Blake's poem, "The Poison Tree."

"August Burial," Saint Teresa de Avila is the source of the line in italics.

"Urn Lake," the recurring phrase, "Lord, it is time," is from Rainer Maria Rilke's poem, "Autumn Day."

"*Horse & Train*" refers to a painting by Alex Colville.

"*How Long Do You Mean to Be Content?,*" a short time before he drowned, Percy Shelley claimed to have encountered his doppelganger who quoted this line from Goethe's *Faust* to him.

Iowa Poetry Prize and
Edwin Ford Piper Poetry Award Winners

1987   Elton Glaser, *Tropical Depressions*
Michael Pettit, *Cardinal Points*

1988   Bill Knott, *Outremer*
Mary Ruefle, *The Adamant*

1989   Conrad Hilberry, *Sorting the Smoke*
Terese Svoboda, *Laughing Africa*

1990   Philip Dacey, *Night Shift at the Crucifix Factory*
Lynda Hull, *Star Ledger*

1991   Greg Pape, *Sunflower Facing the Sun*
Walter Pavlich, *Running near the End of the World*

1992   Lola Haskins, *Hunger*
Katherine Soniat, *A Shared Life*

1993   Tom Andrews, *The Hemophiliac's Motorcycle*
Michael Heffernan, *Love's Answer*
John Wood, *In Primary Light*

1994   James McKean, *Tree of Heaven*
Bin Ramke, *Massacre of the Innocents*
Ed Roberson, *Voices Cast Out to Talk Us In*

1995   Ralph Burns, *Swamp Candles*
Maureen Seaton, *Furious Cooking*

1996   Pamela Alexander, *Inland*
Gary Gildner, *The Bunker in the Parsley Fields*
John Wood, *The Gates of the Elect Kingdom*